Ampersand

Ampersand

poems

by
D. S. MARTIN

CASCADE *Books* • Eugene, Oregon

AMPERSAND
Poems

The Poiema Poetry Series

Cascade Books
An Imprint of Wipf and Stock Publishers
199 W. 8th Ave., Suite 3
Eugene, OR 97401

www.wipfandstock.com

PAPERBACK ISBN: 978-1-5326-4769-7
HARDCOVER ISBN: 978-1-5326-4770-3
EBOOK ISBN: 978-1-5326-4771-0

Cataloguing-in-Publication data:

Names: Martin, D. S. (Don), author.

Title: Ampersand : poems / D. S. Martin.

Description: Eugene, OR: Cascade Books, 2018 | The Poiema Poetry Series.

Identifiers: ISBN 978-1-5326-4769-7 (paperback) | ISBN 978-1-5326-4770-3 (hardcover) | ISBN 978-1-5326-4771-0 (ebook).

Subjects: LCSH: American poetry—21st century.

Classification: PN6110.R4 T87 2018 (paperback) | PN6110 (ebook).

Manufactured in the U.S.A.   02/09/18

In memory of my father,
Ernest William Martin,
(1921—2017)

& of my mother,
Margaret Marie Martin,
soon to depart.

The LORD who created must wish us to create
And employ our creation again in His service
— T. S. ELIOT — *CHORUSES FROM 'THE ROCK'*

Contents

PEAS & QUEUES

& (Ampersand)

What I love about the ampersand is its compactness
& the way it's open to new   & unexpected possibilities
almost forming an eternal figure eight   but not quite
for when the sentence seems to be over
or approaching its end   the ampersand appears
like the first of a hundred thousand well-armed angels
emerging from the backseat of a Volkswagen   & improbable hope
erupts   like a new sunrise   sharply piercing the skin of dark night
with radiating shards of light
& despite the smug sleep   of the ninety nine sheep
when the wanderer's gone   the good shepherd appears
with it draped across his shoulders   & the lost coin
is swept from the cobwebs
& the prodigal stumbles home   where his father watches
& waits   & refuses to lose hope   scanning the horizon
for his returning son   & then he grabs the hem of his garment
& runs   & it's then we recognize the continual pattern
of conflict & resolution   of estrangement & reconciliation
& even of death & resurrection
a pattern that is by no means inevitable   but woven
like the arms of a twisting ampersand
into the fabric of the universe

SAINTS & STUMBLERS

The Twelve

I – Matthew

Yes   I knew Matthew
the best tax collector Capernaum ever had
I know that sounds more like an insult
but it's true   It wasn't his fault
his skills were in demand   & Herod
was willing to pay a good price

He wasn't like the rest Rome usually employs
vermin   sell-outs whose pockets clink
with the fishy stink of dishonest scales
like a monetary meat-cleaver that hacks us

When he threw parties   he didn't notice
the wealthy tisk-tisking his guest list
swelling with the names of the hoi polloi
even those unable to pay their taxes

I was one of the so-called sinners
at his retirement party   when he left
his business to follow Jesus   I laughed
when I heard his young rabbi tell the Pharisees
It isn't those who think they're healthy
who are eager to get well

II – Bartholomew

Can anything good come from Nazareth   from the sticks
from that dotless hick-town on the edge of the map?
I get you   son of Talmai   the one John called Nathaniel
Nothing like that would drop in our laps round here
How can anything good come from Nowhereville
from somewhere even lower than where you're from
from the wrong side of the tracks   the under side
of a stone?   Philip knew you well enough
to find you studying alone   under your fig tree
knew well enough   you weren't mocking prophets
or balking at his mind   so answered
your wonder   *Come & see*
I get you   Bartholomew   No one could fool
you   No naked emperors could pull
invisible wool over your eyes   & so it's all the better
that you were there to watch angels
up & down Jacob's ladder   that you saw
the Christ ascending to the skies

III – Philip of Bethsaida

When my friend questioned me about Jesus
I'd said   *Come & see*   but now realize
that eyes open gradually
that I'd had to start with cloudy shapes
of men like trees walking   like
that man from my hometown   peering
through the spittle

When the Greeks said   *We want to see Jesus*
I grabbed Andrew   fearing my brittle
thread of insight would snap
before knowing what to do   for when
the Master had asked me about buying

the crowd bread   my faith was too little
to say

When we reclined at the table with Jesus
he began to wash our feet   Peter couldn't
see why he'd bother   Thomas tripped
on knowing the way   & I asked him to show
us the Father   His responses were kind
even though   on the eve of his sorrows
we were still so blind

IV – Andrew Son of Jonah

He'd always been my level-headed son
& so I let him wander the wilderness
after his bruised-reed prophet
since he'd always return   to mend the nets
& chase another catch   I'd thought

Simon was the impetuous one
but Andrew was as steady as a boat on sand
When the Baptiser admitted   he wasn't the man
he pointed out the Lamb of God
& Andrew was caught

He followed   & brought Simon
& some other local boys along too
What was I supposed to do?
I only had a fishing life
& he had much more to offer   than I'd got

I only wish it had been when I was young
that Messiah came   not leaving me to fish
& grow old   with the same ache in my bones
my two sons following the unknown
leaving me with naught

V – A Fisherman Called James

The expanse above peers into the depths
Here fishermen reap   as though they're netting
featherless birds   from the blue hills
where cumulus sheep casually drift
Land   sky   & sea   all merge in Galilee
They fish for musht   grip heavy nets
which shimmer   & rip into their hands
drip into water   & into their cedar boat
The sons of Zebedee float   across the face of the deep
lift sails high   dip oars   into the inverted sky
James & his brother grew up on this shore
familiar with the way squalls rip
over the hills   whip up mountainous waves
& how the sea behaves
He knew how bad this storm was
darkness churning   above & below
surges tossing them   as he Peter   Andrew
& John   pulled at the tiny ship's oars like slaves
fearing the spill of water over the gunwale
& so he was all the more startled
when all ceased at his Lord's   *Peace   be still*
& yet   on a similar night crossing   after he got
over the shock   was more able to accept
Christ's walk across those shiny waves
Often   while his ears listened to his Master talk
to the crowds   his eyes would sail
over the Judean hills   that appeared to undulate
like Galilee   bearing boat-shaped clouds   For years
he'd watched bright seabirds easily float
on a breeze that seemed as constant as water
as solid as earth   & so again he was better prepared
when Jesus rose into the sky & disappeared from sight

VI – James the Less

In what way were you less?   Shorter
younger   shyer   than that son of thunder
who shared your name?   Not one to impress
or be given fame   or the one who came
later to the band?   Were you the same James
whose father was Alphaeus   the one whose mother
was a second Mary beneath the cross
the second mentioned among the women
at the tomb?   Would you confess
to taking the blame   to feeling the worst
to seeing yourself whenever he would bless
the least in the kingdom?   Step up James
claim your place   Remember he said
the last shall be first

VII – Simon the Zealot

When I was a child in my father's home
before I was presented at the temple
in the days when Joazar the priest
would have sold us all for peace
Judas the Galilean prevented
such subjection to the hated ways of Rome
Some say he was a brigand when he raided
a palace & armoury   & carried away the gold
After his death his insurrection faded

At first I found another to follow from Galilee
for I was bold to smother the Gentile breath
we breathe   He told us he came to bring a sword
between brothers   but it became a spiritual flame
His authority out-burned the Pharisees
for by his own name he cast out demons
I took on a new zeal   far more real

with true connection to Israel's consolation
For this cause I'd even be sawn in two

VIII – The Judas Tree

Cercis Siliquastrum

From within the alabaster skull of a man
better off unborn
throbs the pressure of regret
The hand that dipped into the bags
    that dipped bread in the dish
    that reached for bloody stars
now scatters to the ground a silver constellation
for the burial of aliens
& strangers

Too late   No return   Too late
The garden's salty kiss of blood
stains his lips   ripe
like Zechariah's prophesy
Irretrievable
as the spikenard of devotion   He grasps
for consolation in the word *friend*

Bloody blossoms hang
from the cursed Judas Tree

IX – Jude

How horrid to live with a tainted name
to be so easily confused   with one who sold your Lord
Who could blame you   Jude
for going by Thaddaeus afterward?
I'm with you   too   in wondering why
Christ wouldn't show himself to the world

Is this why they say you went to Syria
to Libya   to Armenia   to show him yourself?
O patron saint of lost causes
under either of your names
when the iconographers paint you
they show your Pentecostal flames

O Courageous Heart   he said he'd show
himself to those who love him   hiding
behind parables   siding with the dogs
beneath the children's table   & so
you sought to spread that love
as much as you were able

X – Thomas Didymus

When Mary Magdalene said she'd seen
the Lord   it was strangely disappointing
One of the worst women   saved from the street
to have been first   I knew it must be true
that's just what he would do   but then
when I was the only one   to fight fear
& search for myself   the others lagging behind
it was like the soldier's spear   went right through
me too   when I returned to hear
the others bragging   (that was the worst)
that I was the only one   not to have been there
not to have seen where his hands were pierced
I went into denial   *I won't believe*   I said
Anything less than my fingers in his wounds
won't be enough   My words sounded odd
to my ears   A week later I was among
them when he appeared   & called my bluff
My Lord & my God   Conviction rolled off my tongue

XI – Simon Peter

After they'd climbed the hilltop   there came the switch
The scene suddenly defied comprehension   bright
streams of light poured from every pore of the Lord's being
& glistened white from every transfigured stitch
in his clothing   obscuring all else   The others
awestruck   knew enough to listen & watch
but Peter mumbled something asinine   wanting to set
up little shrines for Christ & the two prophets

His tongue often stumbled ahead   He wouldn't let
the Lord wash his feet   & then wanted to be washed
head to foot   He'd follow to the death   he said
but blurted denial to a little servant girl   Yet
he'd stepped over the gunwale into the wake
of their storm-tossed ship   he dove into the lake
to reach Christ on the beach   & put first into speech
the foundation rock that would change the world

XII – John the Beloved

When my brother & I first left our father's nets
who could have predicted this index   of where the Lord
would lead?   Twelve to eleven   to an uncountable
expanse of stars   to Persia   to Egypt   to Rome
to death by sword   by stoning   being sawn in two
beheaded   & crucified   Andrew on an X
cross   & Peter upside down   They each boldly told
of what they'd seen as they died

Domitian tried to silence me   sent me alone to Patmos
where I received a vision of the luminous Word
aglow like pristine snow   & pure gold
encircled by seven lampstands   It was no less
dumbfounding than watching a girl who'd died
being lifted to her feet   no less astounding

than having seen him aglow
with Elijah & Moses on the high hillside

Our understanding was incomplete
We were so numb to wonder   that through his deep
agony in Gethsemane   we actually fell asleep
then waked in panic   & scattered like sheep
whose shepherd's been struck   just as he'd said
we would   As I stood beneath his dying
he assigned me to tend to his crying mother
whose battered heart ached

Like thunder the earth quaked   as noon imitated
midnight   & he became like any other dead man
On the third day I was the one who outran
Peter to the tomb   up in Galilee I was the one
who recognize him on the shore   & I was among
those who watched him rise to the skies
to be seen no more   This is why I was willing to die
or grow to old age   proclaiming the Son of Man

The Camera Lies

484 Waterloo Street, London, Ontario

I had never thought of it as a lie   let alone
of us as conspirators   It's September of 1968
& we're posed on the porch for a photograph

As eldest son   standing straight & still at the centre
of the cluster   I wear a slender tie   probably a clip-on
& stare at the camera until distracted   last second

My kid brother squirms   too young to pretend
but I help preserve the monochromatic illusion
standing on the steps of my great aunt's grand house

14

Portrait With Eyes Turned Aside

I've seen you look into a store window
the way I look into a book
Like you   I begin with what's inside
like you   distracted
when you find your image there
adjusting an errant strand of hair

Any word can form itself
                                    unbidden
into thought
or into a thousand pictures
any image   can be written back
into three-dimensional reality

A good window shows
what you already know
                                    encapsulates
the beauty of our self-conscious world
gives courage to change the things we can
though the wind blows   where it will

Confession

Doing this pleased us all the more because it was forbidden

– Augustine

The truth of the descending sun's rays slants
over glowing hills & growing crops
radiates warmth along the flagstone walk
across the yard   Orange light fills
the town in an instant   spills over rooftops
& the stone wall   that separates my father's orchard
from that of distant neighbours   The beams fall
on a pear tree   that bends under the weight of fruit
& I have no hunger   except to flout the absolute
restriction there before me

Who's to say I can't scale the wall   & nibble a pear
gorge myself till I'm past full   or splatter them there?
The round-bottomed orbs are vulnerable
& the raucous call of my scoundrel friends
makes me dare take chances   to shake branches
& send pears a-thud to the ground   brown bruises
scar their skin where they fall   I don't even care
if I break a few limbs   The audacious sin is mine
We run with a huge load down the road
casting our stolen pearls to hungry swine

Piazza Santa Croce

Protected only by an unwithering wreath of laurel leaves
Dante stands in the full glare of the afternoon sun
his stare   levelled at those who exiled him

from his beloved Florence   He is now a celebrated son
although his marble presence   now a century & a half old
has been shifted from the centre of the square

to make room for a football match   Most tourists don't catch
on he's even there   He towers high above me
one beneath his glance   not even worth banishing
or able to reach to unlatch his boots   from the top stair

Convalescence

At first she did not let the grey-black cloud
weigh her down   Beams burst from the horizon

The sun rose above streaks of grey-black cloud
She watched it   she watched it   then it was gone

There was no sky   only the grey-black cloud
stirred in her coffee   shading her four walls

She began to trust only grey-black cloud
not daring to see the light shining through

I saw the confusion of grey-black   cloud
her mind   for *hope deferred makes the heart sink*

I say this prayer against the grey-black cloud
the deep dark pit   the poison in her blood

Longevity

If a wheel could roll as frictionlessly
as a mass of rock tumbling over & over
through the asteroid belt
circling & circling & circling the sun
it would never slow & never be done
once set in motion   like the one
without stress or strain
riding a pushed wheelchair through a landscape
          without hollow or hill
rolling down
          a never-ending hall
toward a vanishing point   that instead
emerges   expands & gains
the particularity   of door after name-plated door
open wide   so passersby see
into nonagenarians' rooms   each much the same
like the days that roll on & on
into what only seems like eternity

Night–Bound   (John Newton)

I awoke with a shudder   shaken by the howl
of wind in the rigging   the creak of the hull
on the water   the rattle-clank of fetters & chains
Could it really only be   the hollow of the chimney
like some fiendish flute   carved from an old bone
played by my recurring nightmare?   For there's no ship
no night-bound ocean   no crawling hold
despite how sure I was   I'd heard the moan
of dying slaves

        Listen   I told myself   there's the clock
chiming four strokes for the hour   & the clack
of horse hooves on paving stones   The floor doesn't heave
or slope   It's been years since I've been at sea
yet this torment won't leave me   for I have swallowed
the blame   & my belly aches with the shame
of all I have allowed   My outer eyes
have grown dim   & all I now see
is what I coldly saw then

        Shaken   I waken again
Was that the cry of a sick child in the night?
Surely his mother has gone to comfort him
All I can see   is the African infant who wept
uncontrollably   way back when   despite
a mother's arms   only to be silenced when
the angry mate   who'd bought them   swept
him into the sea   The mother then
cried inconsolably

                  I once was lost
in a storm   & cried for mercy as cold water poured
into the hold   Too much a mocker to be so bold
but I prayed to the Lord anyway   The wood was torn
from one side of the boat   & they bound
me to the helm so I could steer   without being washed
overboard   As the men worked the pumps
the cargo shifted & stopped-up the hole
keeping us afloat   I once was lost
the storm lifted   & now I'm found

                                 Right then
I should have abandoned the slave trade
but hadn't yet made the connection   between
my new start   & what I'd seen in the ships   the fear
thumb screws   whips   & degradation
I appeal to the Great Searcher of hearts   before whom
we must all shortly appear   for these haunting memories
of mine have not grown   in my imagination

The Night of Saint Lucy's Day

(with inspiration from Dante, Donne & George Mackay Brown)

Black   the night descends   scarcely seven hours
from when it crept away

Who was this luminous saint   whose legend sings
of faithfulness in the darkest day?

Seven bright leaves in the winter tree
whose roots are frozen   brittle branches thin

Light glitters on the sea   a silver star
an eye plucked out that caused no sin

Night walks with heavy steps
echoes deep loss   the things that are no longer

A child leads her candlelit procession   stronger
than darkness   enabling all to see

Clouds of warm breath   crystallize in the cold
She is the enemy of all cruelty

Cecilia's Song

for the patron saint of music

Cecilia is an unseen moon   Long before
the final forming of my eardrums
I heard   her tidal song
her gentle hum   whispering my name
through iambic thrums
in the warm womb of motherlove
The joy   the sorrow   the birdchirp
of sparrow   the moan of mourning dove
the preludes in the sanctuary
the tunes on the radio   the jungle drums
like a train's rumble through the ground
the sound of a distant flute
like the voice of one crying
prepare the procession route
through the hill country of your soul
they echo her song   & though often unaware
swing open a choice

Cecilia is a watery strait to my drifting boat
beckoning me   not to her
but beyond   her lullaby on rippling air
glimmers with patches of blue skies
She sings me in & out of sleep
breaks with beauty
shakes with light   snags me on deadheads
of wrong & right   Who can despise
those who reach deep   even if they reach

no further   or those who flounder
on the names of God?   She'll bow to no other
despite those who'd smother her song
With larks at break of day
& creatures of the night   Cecilia sings her tune
beneath a suspended   shoulderless moon

Jephthah

In the jingle jangle morning
Jephthah   judge of Israel   came triumphantly home
with clink armour
& clatter carts
his bold vow hardly reconsidered
on the dust-foot   foot-sore march

Well-earned aches sang of victory
bastard days behind
brothers in his debt
his vow a bet against giving his best?   Perhaps
He should never have taken the chance
for first through the front door   plainly seen
the lamb to be slaughtered   his only daughter

Her light-foot celebration dance
& tambourine   with skipping reels of rhyme
in no time   transformed to misery

Leave it to scholars to show Shakespeare
foreshadowing Ophelia's death
Spirit prefiguring Calvary

She walked the hills in a long black veil
a virgin daughter mourning   what would never be
granted two months to roam
The smoke swirl like water whirl
stood   forever   between her   & her wedding day
In the jingle jangle morning
he came stumbling   home

Chasing the Blues

Search for what you've never seen   trace
rumours of the bluesman said to play
in front of that delta five & dime   lug
your microphones and recording machine
to catch & set free an endangered bird
Like grabbing an echo in your hands
grasp in the field what you've never heard
a beauty undervalued in the eye of its holder

Whisper to street corners what versions you know
of the shifting name of Blind Willie McTell
perhaps you'll hear   near some Atlanta hotel
a voice in the wilderness   an insightful guide
leading through the labyrinth of life's hard side
Within his lap   is a dancing twelve-string
& a perfect map   is within his mind
of every blind street he's ever wandered

Strain to hear the hum   of the guitarist
straining strings   over fast fists in an Arkansas
dance hall   A toppling kerosene drum
clangs   flowing flames dance to his rhythm
& the screaming crowd rushes out   He runs
in   for he can't afford to lose   that guitar
now named for the girl they fought over
You follow strange routes   chasing the blues

Instrumental

for Caleb

Like a marionette that doesn't dance
until the puppeteer's fingers
tightly tug her strings

hanging along the wall   strewn about the room
stringed instruments wait   to be retuned
to precision

like birds   on a five telephone-line staff
that perch in silent anticipation
of something to sing about

your mandolin   guitars   & such things
wait   since fingers   such as mine
have not earned their trust

like patient fishing lines   stretched straight
from rod to hook   until the slow tail-swish
brings the magnificent fish along

they wait for your attention   my son
the touch of the one   who loves them
into song

Rembrandt, 1633

As the scaffold is raised   the victim's ribs protrude
Some turbaned figure looks on   as soldiers
struggle with the weight

It's as though death were willing to hesitate
long enough   for Rembrandt to complete
a preliminary sketch

Below the outstretched figure   the artist
in his grey beret   is one of the soldiers
raising the cross

This is well before the loss of his first-born son
the loss of one infant daughter after another
& then his wife

He examined his life with his paintbrush
& despite stumbling in the darkness
was able to shine profoundest light

White Chagall

Oil on canvas, 1938

Christ   ever the suffering servant   serves Chagall
in this depiction   looking down from his sad height

with arms stretched like the wings of a gull
or an albatross   frozen in flight

Flames rise from the synagogue   & the emptied stetl
as soldiers charge to the fight

A man escapes clutching a Torah   & a careful
woman holds a child in her arms   tight

While echoing images of the persecuted   circle
the central figure   awash in heavenly light

his nakedness is wrapped in a prayer shawl
& his halo is discrete   despite

the winds that blow from the scroll
toward the cross   with prophetic insight

The Lord has laid on him the iniquity of us all
for perplexing justice will be proved right

Pietà

St. Peter's Basilica

How young she looks   to have a full-grown son
draped across her knees   Comprehending   we pity

all her face conveys   though the corpse shows
little evidence of his manner of death   Every

vein bulges with life   his muscles maintain their tone
so that his merely human form reflects the divine beauty

in which it was made   & Michelangelo may add knowledge
to skill   from all of those late nights studying anatomy

How young she looks   & how large   but the mountain
of cloth   the genius in the fabric folds   so delicately

shaped from stone   holds our attention & maintains
the pyramid-like balance   We sense the tragedy

of a mother losing her son   & consider all that's known
from scripture   The sculptor expresses his piety

using this most-perfect piece of marble   & his considerable
gift   to speak of love & loss   humanity & deity

How young she looks   as young as the artist's mother
would have been when she slipped into eternity

Figure

after experiencing a Sorel Etrog exhibition

The sculptor's one-legged dancer
      performs on a knife-edge in the still centre of motion
            & his single-stemmed flower
delicately formed   with smooth precision
      blossoms in lean bronze
         as though ephemeral
A herd of cattle heads   as sleek as water-washed stone
      graze under our gaze   A wrench-like bone
         connected to another dry bone   connected
to the horn of a unicorn   as scales of mechanical abstraction
      balance wide   from side to side
         & coalesce as a minotaur skull
The hinges of the heart   whether glistening or dull
      whether burnished   painted   gilded   or oxidized
         speak of hidden chambers
the organic eye-bolts   of how all things consist
      The disparate are unified   twisted & tied
         into metallic knots   the fragile solidified

Passion Suite

I – Mary of Bethany

Some women are blessed with words
I have eloquent tears   My sister weaves
her expectations into reasonable structures
that rise higher than the temple mount
but cannot touch me   for I slip beneath them
stretch my body below them   prostrate
in a flow of spilled emotion   like perfume
from an alabaster jar   that with a quick break
can fill a room

When our brother grew sick   Martha sent word
to fetch the Master   & my prayers leapt
like soldiers in a skirmish   But with our walls
tumbled   & the pillage of our light complete
I stumbled & wept   Though tired
each night I barely slept   Lazarus was dead
There was no need for the mourners Martha hired
though we could afford them   I shed
enough tears for the entire village

When the Lord came   I fell at his feet
& kept repeating what Martha had said
If you'd been here he wouldn't have died
When Jesus cried   I thought he felt the same
despair I did   but then   epiphany
he opened the tomb   as if unwrapping a gift
If you've seen the plume of a fount   you've seen

the lift within me   Skipping over the Mount
of Olives   I danced through Bethany

But whenever I glanced sidelong at the Lord
it seemed a strong cord was ripping
at his heart   I realized his grief was come
& my part would be as some fool
bringing slim relief by sharing sorrow
I poured my prized spikenard on his feet
diluted it with tears   let my hair pool
on the floor   leaving tomorrow to my fears
to serve the one I adore

II – The Procurator's Wife

  I used to be such a sound sleeper   They could condemn
large numbers to death   & torture them under my window in Rome
& I would just slip into deeper slumbers
  Even in the ship   sailing toward this provincial posting
as waves gently rocked me   my breath grew slow & even
while the calm   I now know   mocked me & my naive security
  Since we've come to Jerusalem   I've not felt at home
with smells of sheep & locals roasting meat   I stare as shadows shift
on the ceiling each night   often not finding sleep until first light
  It's more than the strangeness of this place   I keep
seeing the battered face   bashed & bruised   of an innocent man
whose death seems connected to our destiny
  I told Pilate of my dreams   but he refused to listen
boasting he could make the populace meet his demands
& wipe away responsibility   by washing his hands

III – A Servant Girl

The courtyard's cold as bone & the porticos provide
  no shelter   as the day's warmth
    slips into the star-speckled sky

The servants   of those in the Sanhedrin   shiver & wait
        Some soldiers fetch fuel   after they instigate
            the building of a fire   & eye
me with their predatory stare   I'd rather be alone
        but we gather nearby   & stretch wide
            our hands to where heat radiates

Male laughter echoes from stone to stone   I turn
        to investigate a glint within a dark archway
            where orange light touches something metallic
One of the Galilean's followers who had spoken
        with me at the gate   has brought his friend inside
            & now this friend watches the fire burn
Below thick brows his eyes dart as though he's scared to death
        exposing his brokenness   his rabbit-like desire to hide
            I ask   *Were you one of those with Jesus of Nazareth?*

He flees for the cover of words   pretends not to know
        the name   That's when other servants of Caiaphas
            discuss what had happened to Malchus
When some came to capture their lord   one of the disciples
        had whipped out a sword   blood   pain   & a missing ear
            soon restored   I've heard the voice of this Jesus
He's inside now facing pious interrogation   & this disciple's voice
        with its sonorous quality   to us sounds the same
            murmuring like waves splashing a northern shore

A distant rooster crows   & hooves clatter beyond the entranceway
        In the ensuing chatter   we ask him about Jesus again
            but he tries to stress   *I am not one of them*
Weapons clink   as soldiers sway & shuffle to keep warm   Beyond
        the firelight some dark shapes move about   & as the Sanhedrin
            lets out   a few servants are called away
For the third time we confront him   & he calls down a curse on himself
        if he lies   A rooster once more is heard   He looks up
            into the face of Jesus   cries   & flees to outer darkness

IV – The Ravens Fly

a pantoum

I watch three silhouettes   lift to the sky
Toward Golgotha now the ravens fly
A sword would pierce my own soul   it was said
Last week's kingmakers now just want him dead

Toward Golgotha now the ravens fly
Beneath the blare of voices   do stones cry?
Last week's kingmakers now just want him dead
Three men who carry crosses stumble by

Beneath the blare of voices   do stones cry?
I'll ever grieve those streets where he was led
Three men who carry crosses stumble by
The hammer hits each nail on the head

I'll ever grieve those streets where he was led
A sword would pierce my own soul   it was said
The hammer hits each nail on the head
I watch three silhouettes   lift to the sky

V – Salome's Psalm

(at the foot of the cross)

Praise the Lord   O my soul   even when nets
          are empty   & my husband only has
          hired men left in his boat
Praise the Lord   O my soul   despite the hollow-
          heartedness   of having sons walk away
          from their hometown   & their father's trade

For they were chosen to follow the rabbi Jesus
          called from mending nets with their father Zebedee

as boats rocked in the shallows
For they've walked with Messiah himself
         along the wave-washed shore of Galilee
         & the temple courts in Jerusalem

At first I went with our sons   to watch out for them
         but brother could care for brother
         & I too began to see   & to know
My garments gathered dust   in my ambition
         for James & John to gain position
         risking possible jealousy

I was striving after things that have never mattered
         The nails now pull at his flesh
         rivulets of fresh blood stain the wood
Except for my son John   they've all scattered
         so I won't begrudge his giving Mary
         another son   & John another mother

The crown of his kingdom is twined from thorns
         The sky is the dark wing of a crow
         the ground around us   lost in its shadow
Father   into your hands I commit my spirit
         he bellows   It's not just me
         the whole horde can hear it

Even as   all that is within me   mourns
         O my soul   praise the Lord

VI – Mary Magdalene

We followed from a distance   not wanting to stimulate
         false rumour
the others as mothers of those in his band
         me like a sister
with seven reasons to be grateful

I don't expect those not with him to understand
        why we would wait
right to the end   & watch hateful soldiers
        throw dice   slurs
& that final spear into his side

My friend   Mary   gently patted my hand
        as later we watched
to see his burial place   which implied
        we'd bring the spice
& do what was needed once Sabbath was through

As we'd planned   when sun rose we walked in haste
        wondering who
would move that rock so we could go inside
        We were surprised
to find no stone there   & only empty burial clothes

It was not shock   I thought he was the gardener
        before he spoke my name
in his familiar tone   Sometimes we can't see those
        staring us in the face
when we're clinging to our despair

The Castle Church

Shadows fall   where moonlight streams
through arched windows   to form elongated shapes
along the floor   Wasn't that someone knocking on the door?
The sound   or the implication of something equally brave
still echoes through the emptiness   along the night-veiled nave
still echoes centuries after the fire that once brought this building
to the ground   still echoes to the top of the round tower
& right down to the reformer's grave

The rhythmic rap of a hammer has transformed
the droning roll of the Latin tongue   to the vernacular
spoken & sung   *That Word above all earthly powers*
is now perceived   if not understood   The tap
of a nail into wood   even if less than literal
like a foot that keeps time to a beer-hall tune
still echoes down dark aisles   & above an altar
lit by a waxing moon

If the reaction from the Vatican in Rome was   indeed
equal & opposite   the pounding must have been extreme
the sound   & its ninety five points hammered home
It echoes well beyond Wittenberg & Wartburg
has left lasting reverberations high in St Peter's dome
among painted frescoes & stained glass windows
& has reached backwoods chapels   distant grottoes
& wherever the Word is known

Nomenclature

By savouring the precise word
on the back of my tongue   then slowly
rolling it off the tip
is to possess the world
For words are worlds   as Adam knew
as Jacques Cartier also knew
when he made this new world
the land God gave to Cain   naming it
then claiming it   (as though no one lived here)
in the name of the king of France

St Paul's Cathedral

Your statue stands in St Paul's
scorched below your feet   John Donne
by the fire that destroyed much of London
& an earlier cathedral

For one who debated with death
face to face   you were not too proud
to submit   your portrait painted in a shroud
completed weeks before your final breath

This edifice cannot compare with what will be
though your bones shelter beneath its grand dome
Once death is dead   you'll rise to a new home
After one short sleep we'll wake eternally

The Flower of His Ruin

These poems, with all their crudities, doubts and confusions,
are written for the love of Man and in praise of God,
and I'd be a damn' fool if they weren't.

– Dylan Thomas

Once upon a heron-priested shore   where the tide slides
under a chill east wind   a chapel-haunted boy
counting grains of sand   discovered eternity
Before he could ever begin to fathom the mystery
of the ages   the length   & breadth
& depth   & height of love   before the wages
of excess stirred in his whiskeyed blood
or cracked his bones   his naked mind robed itself
in the music of bibles & bards
& waves on wind-washed stones

But the rampages of his father's heresies
& his grim uncle's smudged orthodoxies
drove his spirit over the brink   & down
like a herd of swine   with a legion of reasons to drown
in drink   & stumble the town's blind streets
Once upon a tour of towers & rain
the poet discovered America   which   in turn
discovered him   in the flower of his ruin
leaking in stages across the country
leaving him finally empty   beneath Manhattan sheets

Nothing For It

No point trying to sleep that night
Nothing for it but to rise early
& saddle the donkey   My son after all
was dead   He & I walked
beside the beast   that bore the wood
& the servants   who bore the fire
Something must have betrayed me
for we talked   not at all   till sundown

On the third day I lifted my eyes
to the distant mountain   Here
was where the knife must fall   The rest
was like a dream   I bound my son
who showed complete trust   as I
went through the cold motions of slaughter
but my hand was stayed
& God showed his provision

On the third day   my son who was dead
was raised again

Philippi

Acts 16

Lying in damp darkness every sound is magnified
the clink   clatter & scrape of dragged chains
the drip of distant water

The clop of donkey hooves approaches out in the street
fills this cold stone hole   & then slips away
like a rat through a crack

From deep in the inner cell   a tune begins
Two Jews   who've just been beaten   raise voices
in praise to their god

Such odd behaviour   that keeps us from sleep in this
hopeless place?   *His praise will continually*
be in my mouth

That's when the rumbling begins   dust & debris
earth quake   doors open   fetters break   & each of us
out in the moonlit courtyard

We are too stunned to run   as the wide-eyed jailer
rushes in   a trembling torch in his hand   flames flickering
on his astonished face

The Mind of Alfred Hitchcock

There are many stairways going up
                                   going down
long passageways   curiosity entices you to follow
& uncomfortable winding drives
        where the glare of headlights obscure
as much as they reveal   Every step
      is agonizingly magnified
measured in heartbeats
              & twisted   like the neck
                   of an irrational bird

In the midst of the mundane
                  something cracks
Does it matter   you're both the perpetrator & the victim
neither the perpetrator nor the victim   little more than a voyeur
watching a young secretary   remove her clothes
        through the eyes of an insect
squirming with a compelling fascination
        to be part of the journey
despite deep revulsion & the urge
            to turn away?

Even the camera   veers & lists
      taking your mind with it   since you've given
               him permission
to whisk you where he chooses   Are those
            violins screaming?
What unnatural thing is happening?
           Your mind is possessed

altered en route   by a rational mind
bruised with the ravages of rationality
pushed over the edge

Open your eyes   You're in his dark mind now
where nothing is what it seems
        What do these dreams mean?
Your objections are choked
                by his overwhelming will
        Some blunt instrument comes down
on the interior fingers which hold you in place
        Deep in the vortex is an eye
                There your most secret taintedness
is bluntly exposed

Riel at Batoche

The scout reported   they were marching toward Batoche
Dumont decided ambush   For Dumont it's always ambush
as in the old days   when the herds pounded the prairie
like a hundred thousand of their locomotives   unfettered by tracks
like a swarm of bees swerving left or right as we descend on horseback
like a dry flash flood   beating dust into clouds
for the dark forms of fleeing buffalo to thunder through
    They were marching toward Batoche   having come all the way
from Ontario to Fort Qu'Appelle in just nine days   even with their blasted
railway incomplete   their tired feet trudged through mud
across unfinished sections
    Surround the sleeping soldiers at McIntosh Farm   Dumont decided
& set a wild fire   flames will drive their inexperienced troops into the
mouths
of our flaring gun barrels   two hundred
horsemen will sweep death into their camp
    Gabriel   God has spoken to me   I said
We are to wait   & he will grant victory
    Dumont decided ambush   argued just how outnumbered
we are   how General Middleton's soldiers would pick us off in the open
like calves separated from the herd
but in the bush we have the skills   & know the land   & can wear
them down through ambush
                  as at Duck Lake   where he'd led
the routing of the *invincible* Mounties   & would have chased them
all to their graves   had I not prevented it
                        emboldening the Cree to shed
a little blood themselves
    O the shame that those blind priests should die   who'd rejected

me as the new world prophet   fearing God's word in my mouth
& the days   long past   when I'd found my bed
in a Quebec asylum
        I said
but Gabriel was stubborn   as when he rode south
all the way to Montana   to bring me back to lead the Métis in this rebellion
not listening then   to how I hate bloodshed
or now   how each of Middleton's men wants me dead
because in '70 that braggart Scott had faced our firing squad
        He said I should stay in Batoche   & pray to God
while he led the attack   knowing just the place
in the low   thick woods at Tourond's Coulée
where we'd have cover   & they'd have to cross
like a trapped buffalo herd
        I hear the deep-throated boom of Middleton's field gun
a few miles away   where Dumont has drawn their fire
& have sent all my reinforcements   when the loss
of the Dakotas from our side was reported
My arms stretch in aching supplication for my people   like the arms
of Moses lifted   when Joshua defeated
the Amalekites   a man at either side to hold them higher
although mine form a cross   raised until the victory is won

Memphis, 1968

I've been to the mountaintop   & from there
I've scanned the distance   as far from myself
as the Promised Land

I've been to the motel balcony   over-looking
the parking lot   only able to see dark skies
overhead   the shadow of God's hand

I've seen beyond dark smudges of newsprint
beyond bricks & bottles & broken glass   beyond
mere reactions to reactions

beyond the distractions   & game of turning
cameras from the faults that make you squirm
despite my own infractions

I've seen beyond   to the need for a name
not a man   a voice detached from the sin within
a Moses to lead you   but not enter the land

I've been to the mountaintop   & found
that in secret I've smashed
the tablets to the ground

I've been to the motel balcony   I've lifted my eyes
beyond the hills   to the skies   & seen the glory
of the coming of the Lord

Falling

Stumblers   fall down on their knees
like trees whose roots lose grip in a wind storm

Saints   fall down on their knees
so their spirits & bodies take on the same form

Sometimes it's difficult   from a distance
to tell the difference

Someday   even among the cold & lukewarm
every knee shall bow

PEAS & QUEUES

Notice

Do we ever stop to notice the rightness of organic designs
the broad-leafed maples that grab every raindrop they can
every ray of light   so light that they're almost weightless
extending as far as possible beyond the branches' reach
providing a place for us to escape the heat   & for mosses
& mushrooms to flourish on the forest floor?
Is it coincidence   that their fibres are so fitting
for a builder's needs   for fuel
that their roots prevent soil from washing away
& they breathe out what we need to breathe in?

Do we notice the efficiency of man-made things
the strength of intersecting lines   right angles
within a window frame   dividing four panes of glass
telephone pole after telephone pole stretching across
the prairie   a ship's mast rising above the sea
that practical recurring pattern
builders use when framing a house?
Do you think of its significance
beyond that of structural design   & notice
heaven wink at the coincidence?

The Signpost

Along the gravel shoulder by the guardrail
the wind whips the signpost   & brown-grey grasses
as each transport passes

Every driver has blind spots
concerned with changing lanes or the goal
of his eventual destination

The preoccupied miss the implication
of this arrow   this icon of direction
this serpent lifted upon a pole

O   to simply fulfil this need
to stand   & point beyond myself
a wind-shaken reed

The Hibiscus

As little ones   we are
open-mouthed hatchlings
ravenous & eager

Once we learn to count   we may either
suspect or celebrate the numberless
stars   raindrops   falling leaves

The hibiscus may bloom early
or bloom late   may go from blossom
to blossom   or turn inward
in a deep green silence

Autumn sunlight slants
through the window
Let us accept such grace

Pawns & Queens

From the top of her tower   she sees eight young men
in similar suits   emerging from the base of the building

Like worker bees   she thinks   but they scatter
to their own fields   & not to gather for their queen

Like cogs in my wheel   but she doesn't see
each turning for its own reason   dreaming its own dream

She gives all they could ever want   for a season
until some break free   risking it all on tokens that matter

Approaching Sheol

with thanks to Robert Siegel

Bones creak   like ancient tree limbs in a high wind
the skin   scaly as dried bark
Leaves crackle & crunch underfoot
The movement of the living gives voice to the dead
but slows   like raindrops   the moment before
solidifying on frozen ground
Surrounded by sound   by sound & no sound
there's a shallow dimness in the shadowy grey
Cold   cold   like the thing that isn't
the wind opens its empty mouth
as wide as a tempera scream
What escapes is hunger
There is a place emptier than the grave
a sound emptier than silence

The Sign of the Broken Sword

after G.K. Chesterton

The thousand arms of the forest are grey
its million fingers silver

By moonlight two figures climb a wooded slope
to a frost-etched churchyard

The round priest looks   to be sure a word's
not there

Where would cunning hide a leaf
but a forest?

Where there is no forest   grow a forest
where no darkness   grow a night

Where hide a dead leaf
but a dead forest?

Where hide death   but amongst
the dead?

Like traitors trapped in Dante's lowest pit
a puddle's encased by ice

There is so much good & evil
in revealing secrets

Where would cunning hide a black soul
but a night-veiled forest?

Black Water

You have my heart
                       which is to say
       when you direct harsh words my way
I can't drop the coin of my mind into the deep well
of my occupations   & watch ripples until they fade

        As I look down all I see is darkness
the reflectiveness of the surface has lost its shimmer
& the black water echoes only silence

        I pretend all is well   but the black stars
are distractingly dark   & I can't find a thing in my pockets
not a penny   not a pebble   not a threadbare hole

The Astounded Soul

expanding an analogy from Maurice Manning

When I was a child
prayer was something carefully opened
& closed   a linen closet
with a handle-twist at the outset
& a distinct click   at the end

A poem of iambic precision
with edges folded in   so seams
won't show   every wrinkle
steamed into submission
on the ironing board

But now sheets & pillowcases seem
more at home on the bed   or sailing the line
like Wilbur's swelling angels   flapping bird-like
in the air   with a muted whip-crack
as heard from the boys' changeroom after swim

Some fabrics are for common use
the everyday tablecloth slightly askew
the towel draped over the blue
beach chair   a comfort
when the sun goes in

The formal linen remains unused
behind the door   but the towels & washcloths
uneven   in the bathroom   almost tumbling
to the floor   do what they're called to
Even a poem can rub us clean

Peace & Quiet

      On a crisp   clear suburban morning
where a forest   once yielded to field
which has since yielded   to row after row
of tightly-packed townhouses   amber light
now warms red bricks   & casts long shadows
across the intersection   where peace is submerged
like furrowed farmland when the river rises
as warriors line up   & the battle begins
as with a shout   Right-lane
steers left
      left-lane veers right
throbbing bass taunts all   in the face
of shrill screech   & leviathan roar
      & a cautious mother drives out
for another day's work
where peace will only be caught
if she brought it with her
      The phone rings   so I will know
my mom   at the nursing home
fell out of bed again   last night
so I will know   she's alright
& chaos is kept to a minimum
      & I think of how the quiet & peace
she aspired to   all those years ago
is attained through the dementia
she wraps about her like a fleece
& how   she & I will quietly sit
out in the garden   my voice
carrying only calm & companionship
accepting her silence   as her clear choice

Paris & Quebec

My mind may wander   along the Seine
in Paris   & then within the walls
of old Quebec   or elsewhere
I have been   aided by photographs
or old movie scenes   calling me
with other tourists   to return some day

But more than these   nearby habitations
where I've so often been   but can't
return to   places nothing like they were
renovated   reoccupied   removed
more urgently invite my ambulations
as if their existence in some other realm
depends on me   to maintain the light
at that window   the floorboard
creak overhead   still in my ear
up in that old record store
My expectations are unclear
when I turn my head while driving past
where we used to live   my surprise
unsurprising at oversized trees
that block things I remember   that leave
us only really able to return
to the less familiar   far away

Psalm of Unbroken Bones

About to cry out   like a water-carved cave
a cage of stones   where wind whistles
through narrow cavities
we   your intricate network of bones
      wrapped in tendons & flesh
          stirred by tender breath
we listen   intent to the marrow   in our hollows
for your shouts & groans   that never come
or your acknowledgement
of possible infirmities   that leave us untouched
of all that could be ailing you   but isn't
of what could be bent   but holds form
of every hint of health
      of your unsevered ligaments
      your unpierced skin
      your unshortened days

What if the executioner were to lift you high
causing   what your body weighs
to pull your joints apart   crushing your lungs
straining your heart?   Would you muster
whatever's left   to shout   or cry out
as your rage frays   into grievous moans?
Would you see any better   what treasures you had
as they clatter or drain their separate ways?

We wait   to feel your voice reverberate
      down through each joint   knowing
      it is not our place to initiate praise

to shout   or to make you kneel
We wait   to respond   to raise
         the humerus   elbow   radius & wrist
         to lift high the 27 bones in each hand

We know the beauty of belonging   of connect-
         edness   of what is fitting   of weight
                  balanced on long limbs
We know the rightness of strength   of firmness
         of wholeness   & we wonder
                  if these please you too
We wonder what will get your attention   & wait
                  Might night pierce your bones   pain gnaw
         without rest   your skin drawn thin & tough
as flesh wastes away   so your skeleton protrudes?
                  Might another's suffering be enough
         making your knees knock   the sight
of dry bones scattered across the ground?

                  We feel every sound you mutter
         bone   connected to bone   connected to bone
know   real richness is there to be found
         as wonders flutter
                  through your plainest days   lifting
your mandible skyward   pointing your jaw
         toward the thunder you heard
                  the lightning you saw
         We are the bones that cry out
in unbroken praise

Qualms

Qualm 1

How long   O Lord   will the rooster crow
     from the barn's apex
shout down   drown out   every other voice?

How long will he patrol the barnyard fence
     gather all seed for himself
prevent the hungry creeping through?

Qualm 2

How long will you stay silent   as innocents
     lie dead   & those whose choice
might help   do nothing?   My trust is in you

The stocks rise   & the helpless fall
     They cry out to you
Even those empty of belief   cry out to you

Evanescence

As a kid I pretended I knew   squirmed
in my pre-digital anticipation of the chortled
You don't know   which rubbed my confidence
thin   like threads in my jeans' knee   So now
I look things up   at least words that are new
to me   ones I haven't tricked myself into thinking I know

I tried *evanescence*   thinking it has something
to do with carbonated water   thinking
its essence had simply slipped my consciousness
like the faded inference of navy blue
in my denim jacket   preparing myself
for acquiescence to the dictionary's take on it

I found it means   *the process or fact of evanescing*
or *an evanescent quality*   which makes me want to fling
the dictionary across the room   as unhelpful & over-rated
But before my resolve could vanish   like the smoke
from a wood fire   I read what *evanescence* means
a meaning which   as the book closed   had dissipated

Dreaming the Mississippi

(from Ontario)

     My soul is a river   & I have dreamed
the ancient river   long & deep   It has always wound through me
like veins & arteries   I grew up in another watershed
another nation   but so much desperation always seemed to splash
into its flow   to circle downstream
in eddies around each deadhead
where the sound of the paddle wheeler chugged & churned
through my imagination   & the weeping willow
really had learned to cry   from the sorrow of Johnny Cash
as floodwaters kept rising high from the pouring rain
that I felt I'd earned the right to grieve Mark Twain's
loss   as river town after river town slowly turned
its back on the Mississippi in those years
following the Civil War   having read
the books no one else was reading   & listening
to the music few around me knew   music that grew
out of Dockery Plantation   first picked on a cigar-box guitar
by the likes of Charlie Patton   both the famous & nameless
by hands scarred picking cotton
     I have dreamed   long & deep
from well above John Berryman's Washington Street Bridge
down to the delta   been lulled to sleep
by the story   how it rained & rained
rained both night & day   Lord have mercy   a long time ago
way back in the little town of Tupelo
& without even having left Ontario   I have
headed down into the mystery below   as solo banjo poured

from a well-selected record
　　　　One day we headed west　through an Illinois rainstorm
to visit friends who'd moved to Missouri
But when we crossed the river　it was just a river　& I couldn't dream
ever wanting to dip myself seven times in such a muddy stream
when the rivers of my homeland are much more clean
but　O how I'd dive straight in
if a prophet could send
me　into its legend

Dreaming of Trees

The fog dreams of trees
Their skeletons silently exhale a whiteness that lingers in the morning air

Space loses its clarity
The near becomes distant   The distant ceases to exist

The world is diminished
in the ambiguity of such limited imaginations

Each maple on the boulevard
steps out   in turn   as from behind sheer draperies to introduce itself

The trees dream of fog
forgetfully blurring the edges   like an impressionistic sketch yellowed with age

Belong

How far does it stretch
the astral beam   celestial stream
shimmer-trickle of light
further descended than comprehended
straight from the highest height?
Consider   reduced to a speck in the eye
wheel within wheel   a galaxy spin
The film unwinds faster than our take-up reel
can take it in

Sing heavenly muse
a song to counter the spirit of the age
the rage & rush   the panic & push
the flitter   scamper   clamber cage
the grasp   after what won't last
Sing of the thing that continues
the prolonged   the extended
a song from ancient days
of those whose strength is their length

Long before a white robe covers
northern nesting grounds   the arctic tern
yearns for endless summer   for the long flight
On unseen substance   she hovers
above the globe   chasing light
to the long day   of the antarctic south
She'll obey her goal   pole to pole   swallow
on the wing   what comes to mouth
& follow her long migratory way

Let us honour the patient & insistent
Every great thinker is an imitator
who works & waits   unlike a thief
Every navigator   who considered the birds
of the air   learned from their flight
Every aviator   down the long line
from Wilbur & Orville Wright
shares the benefit of their persistent belief
such things were not absurd

The long   angled stem sticking from the apple
of the earth   helps us grapple to answer
the reasons for seasons
along the tropics of Capricorn and Cancer
& the longer meridians   measure
distance & daylight   & imaginatively
cut orange slices from a blue planet
but the time zone zig-zag   etching such a stone
required a committee to plan it

Praise belongs   to the long   lean giraffe
head in the trees   her long   black tongue
engulfs acacia leaves   Her drumbeat race
& rocking-horse rhythm   imitates
a slow motion grace   through savanna heat
Her hour-young calf   struggles to his feet
waits near for fear   for lions are quick
His mother's leg   long & strong
will dispatch a lion with a single kick

The skip stone   too   shows grace in motion
its thrust & spin
when flung from your finger
for a moment   defies   what must be
We long for perpetual skip across that skin
despite our slight power to throw
but when that stone submits   to sink

think of the long descent
to deep   distant   depths   beyond sight

Fathom that stone at rest in an ocean
cradled in silty hollow   blanketed
by current shift   debris sift
beneath layer after layer   like snow
& the slow juggernaut of geological time
the constant pulse   pace
pull   push   of planet tide
& that stone's eventual climb
to its place in a mountainside

When passing clouds cool   in their long
mountain ascent   & halo the moon
nimbostratus sacks bulge
seams drip   & stitches rip   Patient pine seeds
on the splash-splatter slope   need
root & shoot to strive   Soon (or not soon)
they'll thrive   & grow stronger
since the slow   fight for light
makes full height   take longer

The Trans-Canada Highway   is worth
traversing   The long & winding road
its end   worth waiting for
like the long book   well worth the read
the fish on the hook   reward for an afternoon
& the song worth rehearsing
To sit still on stump   or for long
right on earth   is worth the sight
of that bird   or the deer in the clearing

In anticipation   of moose   elk or deer
we quietly draw near   & sing admiration
of long   strong antlers   patiently regrown
year after year   We sing honour
to the long enduring   a song reassuring

when little may last   Tortoise longevity
can span a century   or two   He never
moves fast   yet reaches his destination
where he suns on his stone

In desert silence   observe the cactus
the one who faces   shadeless blue
the voice of one crying   *Send my roots rain*
In verdant forest   see shadowed maple
the one in places   of blueless shade
sighing for open sky   leaves spread in vain
until new branches curve
toward open spaces   to renew
hope   so dreams won't fade

When passing clouds   roll & shiver
a raindrop may trip aloft or drip
to runnel   stream & river   further
longer than simply to the sea   a process
of constant whirl   A progress
through corn consumed by a cow
or worm used to fish for fish for
a beggar or king   forming as sweat on his brow
wet grows dry   evaporated to the sky

When sailors cross the albatross   suspended
on long wings   they bless the sign
as though it brings   wind on its long flight
& so   there was sorrow in the mariner's crossbow
The great white bird   glides with little loss
of energy   & will shine like a bright cross
as did the apparition   that three times
circled the pine mast   of Caspian's ship
in the form of an albatross

Whatever has strength in its length   whatever
has patience to wait & persevere   celebrate
All that belong   such as those that aspire

to the true   the beautiful   & the good
should be raised in song   such as the redwood
that grows taller than anything on earth
towers with power   & lives long
Of the things that endure   & whose worth
is pure   O heavenly muse   sing

Silver Moon

You have my heart
                    which is similar
         to the moon's grip on this night
Dark branches reach high to embrace the sky
waters bulge   in the curve of an eye

         She slips from behind clouds   & then
slides out of sight   The chapel on the corner stands
secure   stained glass glowing in moonlight

         An unseen violin plays in the dark
I want to love you   like its strings love to sing   like
Christ loves the church   like those windows love the light

Besides the Common Emptiness

Besides the common
in us all
either from the double helix
of my genes
canal or more likely
through childhood
by tides
secretly creating
beneath
before the sink-hole

The hollow holds
a greater-than-normal
to the full measure
& so in me
that burns with unquenchable

emptiness born
    I have another of my own
       of my DNA the code
          before I burst from the birth
         one slowly grown
           like a sea cave worn
            like the washed-out earth
           a cavity
           the road
           swallows an SUV

         a hunger a desire
        susceptibility
      of your worth
    there's a fire
love & loyalty

Glosselle: William Blake

("Auguries of Innocence")

To see a world in a grain of sand
though galaxies fall through our fingers
to find in a name a strong tower
& a heaven in a wild flower

Though galaxies fall through our fingers
secure in the hands of God
though you lose grip on all you've planned
hold infinity in the palm of your hand

Secure in the hands of God
a home where my heart lingers
to find in a name a strong tower
& eternity in an hour

Sightseeing

We look for things we can't see yet
The people of Paris pass on the street
They swirl all around us

You pose on a bridge for a picture
We look down into the Seine's waters
They swirl all around us

The people of Paris pass on the street
The air currents undulate with shadow & light
They swirl all around us

We look down into the Seine's waters
where single moments speak of forever
They swirl all around us

The air currents undulate with shadow & light
as lines waver in Van Gogh's self portrait
They swirl all around us

Where single moments speak of forever
patterns of movement seem motionless as wallpaper
They swirl all around us

As lines waver in Van Gogh's self portrait
we look for things we can't see yet
They swirl all around us

Glosselle: T.S. Eliot

("Four Quartets")

The dove descending breaks the air
descending in time present & time past
The tongues speak of the guilt-bearer
with flame of incandescent terror

Descending in time present & time past
the Word in the desert does not break
From top to bottom the veil will tear
of which the tongues declare

The Word in the desert does not break
following the prepared road from first to last
The tongues speak of the guilt-bearer
the one discharge from sin & error

Dominican Sky   (Higher & Higher)

Puerta Plata

Wind is for billowing   & this bright fabric's
for catching the wind   We sit on the deck
in harness   side by side
where we are the burden   & the burden is light
The tug   like on laundry spread wide
a ballooning blouse   bulging shirt   or swelling sheet
compels us to our feet   & then   casually
lifts us into the air   tethered to a speed boat
cutting through the waves
As line's let out   we rise higher & higher
walking on wind   far above the water
looking down on breakers   the turquoise Caribbean
the shoreline trimmed with sand
& the tip of the mast of an anchored catamaran
Looking up & back at our parachute unfurled
in primary colours against cloudless blue   where we fly
we twist further to see Mount Isabel de Torres
where they say Christ's statue   spreads his arms to the world
the way I picture it will be   when we meet him in the sky

Glosselle: Robert Frost

("Acquainted with the Night")

I have been one acquainted with the night
although I'd never say that we were friends
To avoid the glare   the stillness & the strain
I have walked out in rain   & back in rain

Although I'd never say that we were friends
I recognize our kinship in the dark
the darkness that I keep well out of sight
I have outwalked the furthest city light

I recognize our kinship in the dark
I have walked down to where the harbour ends
To avoid the glare   the stillness & the strain
I have looked down the saddest city lane

November

Niagara-on-the-Lake

October leaves lie on the ground
December chill is in the wind

I stare across the massive lake
toward the tiny point called home

The city glistens in the sun
a speck that sparkles in my eye

The morning mist soon dissipates
as on   day draws me into day

In distant silence freighters move
The waves lap on the stony shore

The arbitrary lines are drawn
Each stone has settled in its place

October leaves lie on the ground
This shore is such a place of peace

But I have promises to keep
I turn away   I turn away

Crossword

Number 1 Down   *a slender shaft shot from
a crossbow*   Pleased to have a good start
Carrie writes   A R R O W

Number 4 Down   *a form of embroidery art*
is   C R O S S-S T I T C H   which will fit
if she makes it a single word

I N T E R S E C T I O N   makes sense
for the clue *crossroads*   sure she won't
have to cross this one out

She wonders about   Number 8 Across
an 8-letter name for   *a game
played by Canada's aboriginals*

Her eyes have trouble focussing   where
the grid bisects   wondering at *beneath
the Jolly Roger's skull*

2 Down   *the gait of a cross country runner*
is probably   J O G   &   R I N G S   seems to be
what's exposed on the cross section of a log

To *double cross* is a form of
B E T R A Y A L   & *a brutal Roman
execution*   is   C R U C I F I X I O N

but she becomes angry at each missed solution

86

& when   a ten-letter word   meaning   *to buy back*
or to have a debt crossed out   seems out of reach

Tintern Abbey

Even in the rain   the ruin
of Tintern Abbey is like the ornate frame
of a painting in the Louvre

Gothic windows contain the wooded green hills
in a series of architectural shapes
whose content shifts & fills
as we draw nigh & as the mist moves
From its height   sharply outlined tracery
understands the subtle possibilities of such light

Great sandstone arches   lifted
for glory & honour & praise   contextualize
the moody grey skies

The King's Highway

I'm calling on you to fire up your chainsaws
load the dynamite   & cut a line   straight
as the crow flies   Every hollow needs to swallow
the neighbouring hillside   The weight of all
that granite needs to be humbled   to tumble
from the highest height   to the lowest low
The clang & rumble of your bulldozer
will be given free rein as you shove
rock   rubble   gravel   & sand to make smooth
the way

Will you span deep valleys   without the slightest
deviation in direction   slice wooded rock cuts
give all you've got   to be the juggernaut
shot straight through the pine forests of your days
with not a curve to steer   or peer around?
Every valley shall be exalted   raised   lifted up
& the granite hillsides razed   brought low
& the crooked made straight   the crooked straight
levelling the landscape   flattening whatever stands in
the way

The Soul as a Grocery Cart

Imagine the soul as a grocery cart
a little less than ok
in the parking lot corral
a little weather-stained from rain
& snow   a little wobbly in the wheels
a little bent in the frame   a little worse for wear
since its glistening start

It's not so strange   seeing your soul
as a grocery cart   perhaps best understood
as the receptacle of your being
So as you attempt to gauge the contents
of its silver cage   what hard-won attainments
have fallen through its holes   what good
has you wondering where it went?

As you push this part of yourself about
through miles of aisles   acquiring
the desires of your heart
which of your accoutrements would you rate
as better placed back on the shelf
before you navigate your soul to the final checkout
before the cashier examines what's in your cart?

Acknowledgements

Thank you for buoying me through the writing of this collection — friends, fellow poets, and encouragers from a distance. I am thankful for the privilege of being Series Editor for the Poiema Poetry Series. (How can I express how amazing it is to assist such gifted and humble artists?) I am thankful to have been embraced by the community of McMaster Divinity College. I am thankful for the enrichment and support of my well-loved family, and so many friends. Appreciation also goes to Richard Greene for help in the editing process — of course to the writing group that meets in our home (you have often been the first audience and flaw-fixers for these poems) — and to the editors of the following publications, where many of these poems first appeared, sometimes in slightly different forms. Praise God from whom all blessings flow.

Soli Deo Gloria — DSM

Anglican Theological Review — "James The Less"

Altarwork — "Jude," "Simon the Zealot," "Mary of Bethany"

Carousel — "Approaching Sheol"

The Christian Century — "Andrew Son of Jonah," "Thomas Didymus"

Christianity and Literature — "Night-Bound" ("This work originally appeared in *Christianity and Literature*. Reprinted with permission.")

Crannóg — "The Night of Saint Lucy's Day"

The Cresset — "A Fisherman Called James," "Simon Peter"

Crux — "Salome's Psalm"

The Dalhousie Review — "The Astounded Soul"

Flourish — "Belong"

In Touch — "Nothing For It," "Falling"

Letters — "Matthew"

MiPoesias — "Sightseeing"

The Other Journal — "Portrait with Eyes Turned Aside"

Perspectives — "Silver Moon"

The Prairie Journal of Canadian Literature — "Riel at Batoche"

Presence — "St Paul's Cathedral"

Queen's Quarterly — "Nomenclature"

Sehnsucht — "The Sign of the Broken Sword," "Tintern Abbey"

Seminary Ridge Review — "Glosselle: William Blake"

Sojourners — "& (Ampersand)"

The Southern Quarterly — "Dominican Sky"

Spadina Literary Review — "Besides the Common Emptiness"

Spiritus — "Notice"

Stonework — "Chasing the Blues," "The Signpost"

Studio — "The Judas Tree"

Swept Media — "Longevity," "Instrumental"

The Toronto Quarterly — "Glosselle: T. S. Eliot," "Glosselle: Robert Frost"

Vineyards — "The Hibiscus," "Dreaming of Trees"

Windhover — "Piazza Santa Croce," "Convalescence," "The King's Highway," " The Soul as a Grocery Cart"

Windsor Review — "November"

Poems in this collection have also previously appeared in the following anthologies: *Down to the Dark River: Contemporary Poems about the Mississippi River* ©2016 Louisiana Literature Press — "Dreaming the Mississippi"; *Adam, Eve, & the Riders of the Apocalypse* ©2017 Wipf & Stock Publishers — "James the Less," "Thomas Didymus," "Jephthah," "Nothing For It," "Philippi."

"The Judas Tree" also previously appeared in my collection *Poiema* ©2008 Wipf & Stock Publishers.

Collections in this Series Include:

Six Sundays toward a Seventh by Sydney Lea

Epitaphs for the Journey by Paul Mariani

Within This Tree of Bones by Robert Siegel

Particular Scandals by Julie L. Moore

Gold by Barbara Crooker

A Word In My Mouth by Robert Cording

Say This Prayer into the Past by Paul J. Willis

Scape by Luci Shaw

Conspiracy of Light by D. S. Martin

Second Sky by Tania Runyan

Remembering Jesus by John Leax

What Cannot Be Fixed by Jill Peláez Baumgaertner

Still Working It Out by Brad Davis

The Hatching of the Heart by Margo Swiss

Collage of Seoul by Jae Newman

Twisted Shapes of Light by William Jolliff

These Intricacies by Dave Harrity

Where the Sky Opens by Laurie Klein

True, False, None of the Above by Marjorie Maddox

The Turning Aside anthology edited by D.S. Martin

Falter by Marjorie Stelmach

Phases by Mischa Willett

Second Bloom by Anya Krugovoy Silver

Adam, Eve, & the Riders of the Apocalypse
anthology edited by D.S. Martin

Your Twenty-First Century Prayer Life by Nathaniel Lee Hansen

Habitation of Wonder by Abigail Carroll

Ash & Embers by James A. Zoller

Full Worm Moon by Julie L. Moore (forthcoming)